SUPER**SPORTS**
INFOGRAPHICS

SUPER
BASKETBALL
INFOGRAPHICS

Jeff Savage

graphics by
Rob Schuster

Lerner Publications • Minneapolis

Copyright © 2015 by Lerner Publishing Group, Inc.

All rights reserved. International copyright secured. No part of
this book may be reproduced, stored in a retrieval system, or
transmitted in any form or by any means—electronic, mechanical,
photocopying, recording, or otherwise—without the prior written
permission of Lerner Publishing Group, Inc., except for the inclusion
of brief quotations in an acknowledged review.

Lerner Publications Company
A division of Lerner Publishing Group, Inc.
241 First Avenue North
Minneapolis, MN 55401 USA

For reading levels and more information, look up this title at
www.lernerbooks.com.

Main text set in Univers LT Std 12/15.
Typeface provided by Adobe Systems.

Library of Congress Cataloging-in-Publication Data

Savage, Jeff, 1961–
     Super basketball infographics / by Jeff Savage ; illustrated by
Rob Schuster.
       pages   cm. — (Super sports infographics)
     Includes index.
     ISBN: 978-1-4677-5233-6 (lib. bdg. : alk. paper)
     ISBN 978-1-4677-7575-5 (pbk.)
     ISBN: 978-1-4677-6276-2 (EB pdf)
     1. Basketball—Graphic methods—Juvenile literature.
I. Schuster, Rob, ill. II. Title.
GV885.1.S28 2015
796.323'021—dc23   2014011000

Manufactured in the United States of America
1 – DP – 12/31/14

CONTENTS

GOING TO COURT

Are you a basketball fanatic? To find out, take this quiz.

1. Do you ever wonder about the average height of basketball players in the National Basketball Association (NBA)?

2. Do you want to know who has won the most NBA championships?

3. Are you curious about who's the highest-paid player in the NBA?

4. Looking for a way to gauge your chances of playing in the NBA?

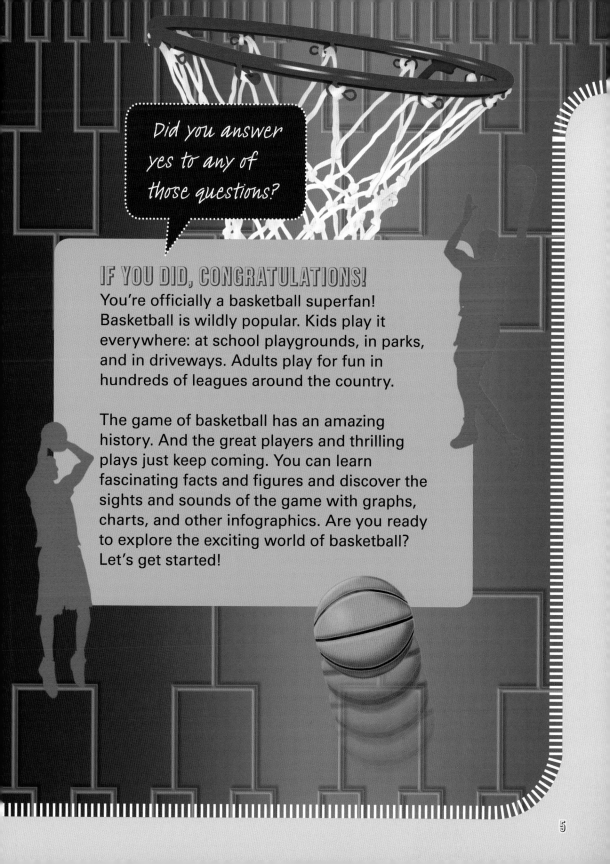

Did you answer yes to any of those questions?

IF YOU DID, CONGRATULATIONS!

You're officially a basketball superfan! Basketball is wildly popular. Kids play it everywhere: at school playgrounds, in parks, and in driveways. Adults play for fun in hundreds of leagues around the country.

The game of basketball has an amazing history. And the great players and thrilling plays just keep coming. You can learn fascinating facts and figures and discover the sights and sounds of the game with graphs, charts, and other infographics. Are you ready to explore the exciting world of basketball? Let's get started!

SPANNING THE GLOBE

James Naismith invented basketball in Springfield, Massachusetts, in 1891. Since then, the sport has gone global. Professional leagues are found worldwide. But many pros want to come to the United States to play. After all, the NBA is the highest-paying basketball league in the world. The 2013–2014 season featured a record-breaking 92 players from 39 countries outside the United States, as shown on the map below.

Canada
8

United States
268

Mexico
1

Haiti
1

Dominican
Republic
2

Puerto Rico
1

US Virgin Islands
1

Venezuela
1

Brazil
4

Argentina
4

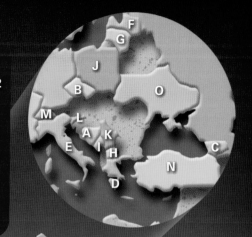

Key to Magnified Area

A Bosnia and Herzegovina 2
B Czech Republic 1
C Georgia 2
D Greece 1
E Italy 4
F Latvia 1
G Lithuania 2
H Macedonia 1
I Montenegro 2
J Poland 1
K Serbia 2
L Slovenia 2
M Switzerland 1
N Turkey 4
O Ukraine 2

Sweden 2

Germany 3

Great Britain 2

France 10

Spain 5

Russia 4

Israel 2

Senegal 2

Nigeria 1

Democratic Republic of the Congo 1

Cameroon 1

Congo 1

Tanzania 1

Australia 5

New Zealand 1

WILL YOU GO PRO?

Do you dream of playing in the NBA? You will need to beat the odds. Check out the number of players in the United States at each level of the sport in 2013. You will see just how rare it is for an amateur basketball player to make it to the top pro leagues in the United States.

Girls

There were 1,090 colleges featuring women's basketball teams in the United States in 2013.

The Women's National Basketball Association (WNBA) has 12 teams with 12 players on each team.

Pro players 144

College players 16,186

High school players 433,120

There were 17,493 high schools in the United States with at least one girls' basketball team in 2013. Only 1 in 3,008 girls' high school players makes it to the pros.

Boys

Pro
Players
360

The NBA has 30 teams with 12 players on each roster.

**College players
17,984**

Colleges around the United States supported 1,071 men's basketball teams in 2013.

High school players
538,676

In 2013, there were 17,856 high schools in the United States that had one or more boys' basketball teams. Only 1 in 1,496 boys' high school players makes it to the pros.

GETTING INTO THE GAME

In March, sports fans are glued to the TV to watch the National Collegiate Athletic Association (NCAA) men's basketball tournament. The NBA Finals in June draws another huge audience. Check out these figures from 2013 to see how many viewers watched basketball's biggest games compared to other major sporting events.

19.2 million viewers

16.2 million viewers

16.7 million viewers

8.2 million viewers

KEY
One

equals
1 million
viewers

Stanley Cup Finals Game 6

Kentucky Derby

Daytona 500

World Series Game 6

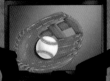

Chicago Blackhawks versus the Boston Bruins

Boston Red Sox versus the St. Louis Cardinals

23.4 million viewers

26.3 million viewers

26.4 million viewers

108.7 million viewers

NCAA basketball championship

NBA Finals Game 7

NCAA football championship

Super Bowl

University of Louisville versus the University of Michigan

San Antonio Spurs versus the Miami Heat

University of Alabama versus the University of

Baltimore Ravens versus the San Francisco 49ers

MARCH MADNESS

The NCAA basketball tournament is so popular partly because fans never know who is going to win the title. First, teams have to make it into the tournament by playing well during the regular season. Of the 346 Division I college teams, only 68 earn a spot. Then a team has to win all its games in the tournament and be the last team standing. The odds are not good. Imagine winning the championship more than once! Only 14 coaches have led their teams to multiple championships. Here are the most successful coaches in NCAA history.

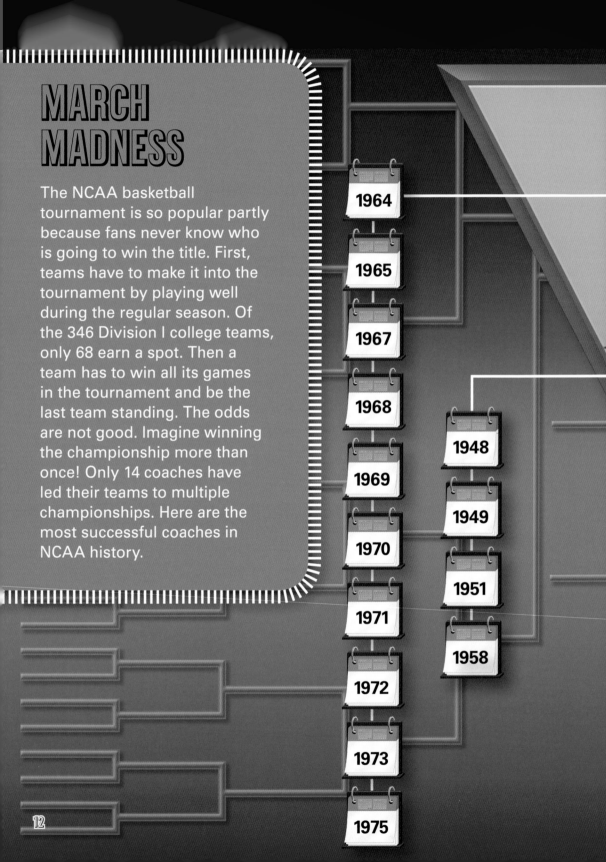

1964

1965

1967

1968

1948

1969

1949

1970

1951

1971

1958

1972

1973

1975

JOHN WOODEN
University of California, Los Angeles (UCLA)
10 NCAA championships

ADOLPH RUPP
University of Kentucky
4 NCAA championships

MIKE KRZYZEWSKI
Duke University
4 NCAA championships

JIM CALHOUN
University of Connecticut
3 NCAA championships

BOB KNIGHT
Indiana University
3 NCAA championships

Nine coaches
tied with
2 each

1991

1999

1992

1976

2004

2001

1981

2011

2010

1987

HEY, UP THERE! (HELLO, DOWN THERE)

Fans know that most pro basketball players are taller than the average person. But some players even tower over their own teammates. And a few players are tiny compared to everyone else on the court. Here are the tallest and shortest players in NBA history who played at least three years in the league.

SPUD WEBB
5 feet 6 inches
(1.68 m)
(1985–1996,
1997–1998)

GREG GRANT
5 feet 7 inches
(1.70 m)
(1989–1993,
1994–1996)

EARL BOYKINS
5 feet 5 inches
(1.65 m)
(1998–2008,
2009–2012)

KEITH JENNINGS
5 feet
7 inches
(1.70 m)
(1992–1995)

YAO MING
7 feet 6 inches
(2.29 m)
(2002–2009,
2010–2011)

MANUTE BOL
7 feet 7 inches
(2.31 m)
(1985–1994)

GHEORGHE
MURESAN
7 feet 7 inches
(2.31 m)
(1993–2000)

SHAWN BRADLEY
7 feet 6 inches
(2.29 m)
(1993–2005)

AVERAGE NBA
PLAYER IN 2013
6 feet 7 inches
(2.01 m)

AVERAGE US MAN
IN 2013
5 feet 8 inches
(1.73 m)

TYRONE
"MUGGSY"
BOGUES
**5 feet
3 inches**
(1.60 m)
(1987–2001)

SCORING FRENZY!

What team scored the most points in a single NBA game? The answer is more complicated than you might think. Some games go into overtime. The extra time can help teams score a ton of points. For instance, in 1983, the Detroit Pistons beat the Denver Nuggets, 186–184. But that game included three overtime periods. Check out this graphic to see the five highest team point totals of all time in a game that didn't go into overtime, broken down by scoring per quarter.

MARCH 12, 1970
Cincinnati beat the San Diego Rockets, 165–151

MARCH 16, 2008
Denver beat the Seattle SuperSonics, 168–116

38

41

38

43

43

36

46

48

CINCINNATI ROYALS

DENVER NUGGETS

MARCH 2, 1962

**Philadelphia beat
the New York
Knicks, 169–147**

NOVEMBER 10, 1990

**Phoenix beat the
Denver Nuggets,
173–143**

FEBRUARY 27, 1959

**Boston beat the
Los Angeles Lakers,
173–139**

PHILADELPHIA WARRIORS	PHOENIX SUNS	BOSTON CELTICS
44	26	52
46	40	38
37	57	43
42	50	40

MOST VALUABLE PLAYERS

Have you ever heard of Maurice Podoloff? Many basketball fans haven't. He was the first commissioner of the NBA, and the league's most valuable player (MVP) trophy awarded at the end of each season is named for him. But while you probably don't know the name Podoloff, the names of the greatest basketball players of all time may be more familiar. Here they are, as measured by the number of times each player has been named NBA MVP as of 2013.

WILT CHAMBERLAIN
4

LEBRON JAMES
4

MAGIC JOHNSON
3

LARRY BIRD
3

KAREEM ABDUL-JABBAR

6

BILL RUSSELL

5

MICHAEL JORDAN

5

MOSES MALONE

3

WONDERS OF THE WNBA

Women have been playing basketball since shortly after the game was invented. But the first professional women's league wasn't formed until 1978. It lasted three seasons. Several more pro leagues came and went. The WNBA began play in June 1997. Since then, eight different teams have won the WNBA championship at least once. Take a look at these graphics to see all the WNBA playoff teams from the last few years. The team in the middle was the champion.

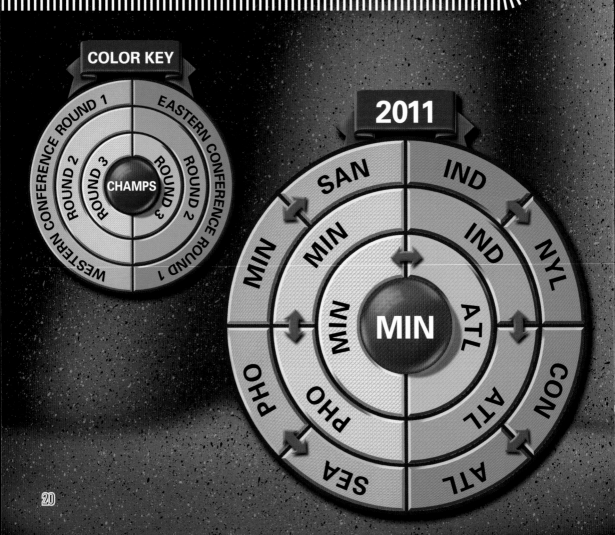

COLOR KEY

WESTERN CONFERENCE ROUND 1
ROUND 2
ROUND 3
CHAMPS
ROUND 3
ROUND 2
EASTERN CONFERENCE ROUND 1

2011

SAN
MIN
MIN
IND
IND
NYL
MIN
MIN
MIN
ATL
CON
PHO
PHO
ATL
ATL
SEA

2012

MIN
CON
SEA
MIN
CON
NYL
IND
MIN
IND
IND
LAS
LAS
IND
SAN
ATL

2013

MIN
WAS
SEA
MIN
ATL
ATL
MIN
MIN
ATL
IND
LAS
IND
PHO
CHI
PHO

SEEING DOLLAR SIGNS

If you make it to the NBA, you're on your way to becoming rich! Pro basketball players have always made pretty good money. And over time, because of inflation (increasing prices for goods and services), paychecks have continued to grow. But as the sport has gotten more popular around the world in recent years, salaries—the amounts athletes earn per year—are off the scale. Check out the top 10 salaries in the NBA for the 2013–2014 season.

Dwyane Wade	LeBron James	Chris Bosh	Pau Gasol	Dwight Howard
$18,673,000	$19,067,500	$19,067,500	$19,285,850	$20,513,178

Key

equals
$1 million

Carmelo
Anthony
$21,388,953

Joe
Johnson
$21,466,718

Amar'e
Stoudemire
$21,679,893

Dirk
Nowitzki
$22,721,381

Kobe
Bryant
$30,453,805

23

GETTING INTO POSITION

What was the average height of NBA players at each of the five positions in 2013–2014? Take a look at this graphic to find out. You can also see where each position generally plays on the court during a game.

POINT GUARD
6 feet 2 inches
(1.88 m)

SHOOTING GUARD
6 feet 5 inches
(1.96 m)

SMALL FORWARD
6 feet 8 inches
(2.03 m)

POWER FORWARD
6 feet 9 inches
(2.06 m)

CENTER
6 feet 11 inches
(2.11 m)

Power forwards play near the basket and need to be able to score and grab rebounds.

Centers are usually the tallest players on basketball teams. They stay close to the basket to score, grab rebounds, and block shots.

Shooting guards are mainly responsible for scoring and must be able to do so from anywhere on the court.

Small forwards play closer to the basket than guards, but they should be good shooters who can hit outside shots as well.

Point guards usually play far from the basket and direct their team's offensive attack and try to make assists.

RECORD PERFORMANCES

Records are meant to be broken. But a record that seems out of reach in the NBA is Wilt Chamberlain's record of points in a game by a single player. Chamberlain, a center, was a powerful 7 feet 1 inch (2.16 m) tall at a time when most other players were several inches shorter. As a result, he dominated the league for more than a decade.

Nov. 15, 1960

Dec. 8, 1961

Jan. 13, 1962

March 2, 1962

Nov. 3, 1962

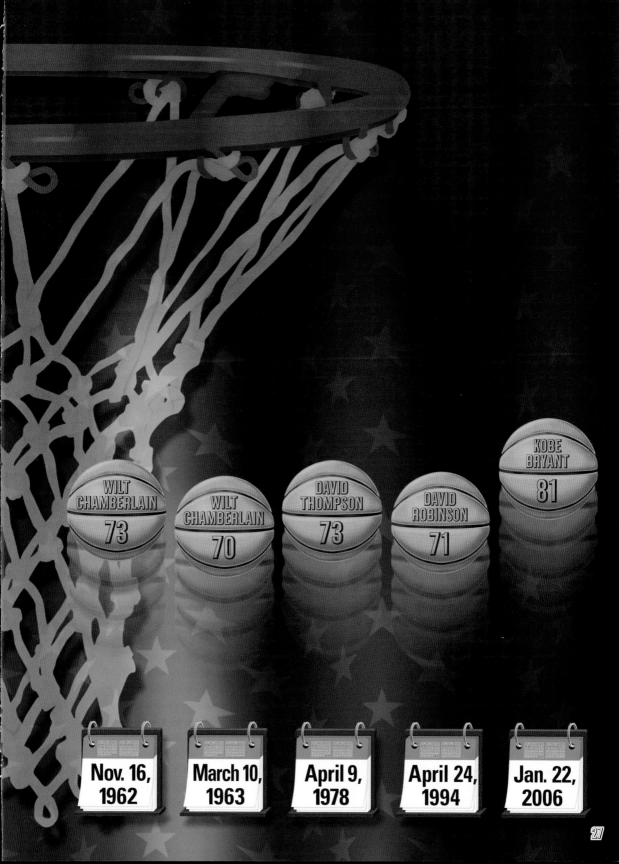

WILT CHAMBERLAIN 73

WILT CHAMBERLAIN 70

DAVID THOMPSON 73

DAVID ROBINSON 71

KOBE BRYANT 81

Nov. 16, 1962

March 10, 1963

April 9, 1978

April 24, 1994

Jan. 22, 2006

WHO ARE THE CHAMPIONS?

Since 1946, when the NBA started, 18 teams have hoisted the championship trophy. (For the first three seasons, the league was called the Basketball Association of America.) Each year, 30 teams battle to reach the playoffs. The winning team of each series advances to the next round, while the losing team goes home. Finally, only two teams remain. They battle in the NBA Finals to see who will be champion. Take a look at the most successful teams in NBA history. The numbers inside the basketballs show how many times each team won the Finals. The years on top of the trophy cups show which years they won.

Dwyane Wade led the Heat's first title-winning team, and LeBron James joined Wade for the next two titles.

Isiah Thomas led the way to the Pistons' first two championships.

The Warriors won their first two titles in Philadelphia and their third in Oakland, California.

Hakeem Olajuwon was the Finals MVP both times.

Walt Frazier and Willis Reed starred in the 1970s.

Houston Rockets	New York Knicks	Miami Heat	Golden State Warriors	Detroit Pistons
		2013	1975	2004
1995	1973	2012	1956	1990
1994	1970	2006	1947	1989
2	**2**	**3**	**3**	**3**

The Celtics won eight titles in a row.

The Lakers won their first five titles in Minneapolis before moving to Los Angeles in 1960.

All six championships starred Michael Jordan.

The 76ers won their first title in Syracuse, New York, before moving to Philadelphia in 1963.

Tim Duncan was the team leader for all five.

Philadelphia 76ers	San Antonio Spurs	Chicago Bulls	Los Angeles Lakers	Boston Celtics
				2008
			2010	1986
			2009	1984
			2002	1981
			2001	1976
			2000	1974
			1988	1969
			1987	1968
			1985	1966
			1982	1965
			1980	1964
		1998	1972	1963
	2014	1997	1954	1962
	2007	1996	1953	1961
	2005	1993	1952	1960
1983	2003	1992	1950	1959
1967	1999	1991	1949	1957
1955				

Philadelphia 76ers	San Antonio Spurs	Chicago Bulls	Los Angeles Lakers	Boston Celtics
3	5	6	16	17

Glossary

AMATEUR: an athlete who is not paid to play a sport

ASSIST: to pass the ball to a teammate who then scores a basket

COMMISSIONER: the person in charge of an organization, a business, or a department

DAYTONA 500: the biggest NASCAR race of the year, held at Daytona International Speedway in Daytona Beach, Florida

DIVISION I: the top level of NCAA athletics

DOMINATE: to control or have a huge influence over

INFLATION: an increase in prices and a decline in the value of money

KENTUCKY DERBY: one of the most famous horse races in the world. The race is held each spring at Churchill Downs in Louisville, Kentucky.

NATIONAL COLLEGIATE ATHLETIC ASSOCIATION (NCAA): an organization that oversees organized sports at the college level

OVERTIME: an extra period to be played when a game ends in a tie. If the game remains tied after overtime, a second overtime is played and so on.

REBOUND: to grab or otherwise gain hold of the ball after it is shot at the basket

SALARY: a fixed payment that is made on a regular schedule in exchange for doing a job

Further Information

Coy, John. *Hoop Genius: How a Desperate Teacher and a Rowdy Gym Class Invented Basketball.* Minneapolis: Carolrhoda Picture Books, 2013. Find out more about the man who invented basketball.

Fishman, Jon M. *Kevin Love.* Minneapolis: Lerner Publications, 2014. Learn how Kevin Love has succeeded at every level of basketball.

HoopsHype
http://hoopshype.com
This popular site offers the latest news about basketball from the NBA, college conferences, and minor and international leagues.

Inside Hoops
http://www.insidehoops.com
This cool site provides fans with up-to-the-minute basketball information from polls, videos, blogs, tweets, and other sources.

Kennedy, Mike, and Mark Stewart. *Swish: The Quest for Basketball's Perfect Shot.* Minneapolis: Millbrook Press, 2009. This book takes readers beyond the statistics and explores the history, biggest moments, and much more about the sport of basketball.

NBA
http://www.nba.com
The official NBA website provides fans with game results and biographies of players and is loaded with statistics like those found in this book!

Nbadraft.net
http://nbadraft.net
This site features the top high school and college players, discusses their strengths and weaknesses, and predicts their place in the NBA draft.

Savage, Jeff. *LeBron James.* Minneapolis: Lerner Publications, 2014. Read about the life of the best basketball player in the NBA.

Sports Illustrated Kids
http://www.sikids.com
The *Sports Illustrated Kids* website covers all sports, including basketball.

Wilner, Barry. *Basketball's Top 10 Scorers.* Berkeley Heights, NJ: Enslow Publishers, 2011. Compare great scorers of the past to today's highest-flying basketball superstars.

Index

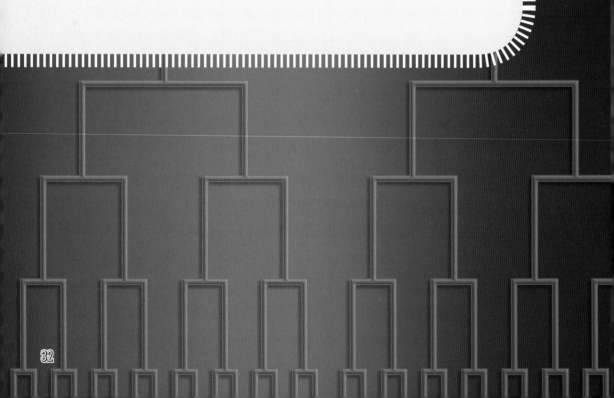